CHAMELEON
AURA

CHAMELEON
AURA

BILLY CHAPATA

Andrews McMeel
PUBLISHING®

there is something quite **magical** about looking within and realizing that all the power you need to re-create yourself, lies within. there is something quite **revolutionary** in understanding that the keys to your peace, your emancipation, and your happiness all rest comfortably in your pocket.

as we proceed on this journey called life, we will take on many **shapes**, many **forms**, and many **identities**, and this is what makes us truly beautiful. the experiences we go through, and the people we cross paths with, only add more energy to the direction we're headed in, more detail to the ground that we step on, and more **color** to our narrative.

we will **heal**, and our auras will transform.

we will **grow**, and our auras will change.

we will **love**, and our auras will illuminate.

here's to healing, here's to growing, here's to loving, and here's to hoping that these words keep your aura bright and **colorful**.

CONTENTS

cerulean. 1

amaranth. 69

mikado. 139

viridian. 207

metamorphosis. 277

cerulean.

repeat this in the mirror every day until it resonates:

i am not flawed,

i am not flawed,

i am **misunderstood magic**.

**law of attraction.**

attract love, don't chase it.

spread love, and it will flow back to you like ocean waves.

<u>*unique.*</u>

i was meant to be **experienced** differently.

i am not a friend you've had before,

i am not a lover you've loved before,

i am **me**.

reflections in the mirror.

look at how far you've come over the years. look at the relationships you've gained and lost. **reflect** on your growth.

look at what you still hold on to. what serves you and what doesn't? is it still **conducive** to you or does it poison you?

shift your attention to things that bring out the **light** in you. things that grow you, things that make your soul **smile**.

reflect, **release**, and **reenergize**.

<u>**unpaid debts.**</u>

you owe yourself the same love you gave old lovers,

who couldn't love you with the same intensity
while your soul **starved**.

(your growth is all about you)

there are older versions of you that only **exist** because other people give them oxygen, and you are not obligated to keep those versions **alive** to make other people happy.

<u>*surface-level lovers.*</u>

there are some who will only be able to comprehend you on the
surface, and be completely unable to dive into the depths you have
to offer. there are some who will be fascinated by the oceans
within you, and be unable to swim in the waves you give off.
do not settle for mediocrity.

weaknesses.

your **intensity** to love is not a weakness. detach yourself from anyone who misunderstands your passion and pours water onto your flame.

your **willingness** to forgive is not a weakness. when your compassion is used against you, show yourself compassion and walk away.

your **ability** to remain soft is not a weakness. don't let life harden your soul. there is strength and bravery in vulnerability.

<u>*pied piper.*</u>

i no longer have the desire to explain myself.

my vibrations may be too **intense** or too **gentle** for some,

but i will move to my own tune.

(things the universe taught me)

the **truth** is in the energy.

energy is in the **truth**.

darling,

heal at your own pace. don't be rushed into connections by
individuals who are not willing to pour **honey** over your wounds.

<u>your way.</u>

healing is not an overnight process. wounds will **reopen**, wounds
will **close**, but always allow yourself to feel what you feel. we are
consumed by the idea that negative emotions aren't conducive,
that we must suppress darkness, but growth comes from being
uncomfortable. you may have to take a few steps back to move
forward, open old wounds to make way for new memories, but
this is necessary.

trust your process.

(conversations with self)

trust me, i got you.

—intuition

(i have learned to separate from those shrouded in ambiguous and unclear intentions, because it will cause you to be unsure of yourself. when you know your worth, you'll stop entertaining those who don't know what they want. you deserve clarity and directness. demand it)

i'm all for **loud** intentions.

intentions so loud they **silence** any doubts.

intentions so **clear** you can see right through them.

honest energy.

fully.

and when you love her,

don't just love her **petals**,

love her **thorns** too.

<u>consistency.</u>

i don't swim in inconsistent energy for long.

i don't like waves that are **heavy** some days,

and **soft** on others.

be **fluid** with me throughout.

intact.

she's mastered the

art of giving pieces of

herself to the world,

while remaining whole.

self-love is the **glue**

that keeps her together.

(lessons old lovers taught me)

true love is never hidden,

but **ego** creates the best hiding spots.

.

letters that hypermasculinity was afraid to send:

i wasn't ready for you.

it wasn't that the feelings for you weren't there. it wasn't that
my heart wasn't warmed by every breath you took. it wasn't that
the love i had for you was momentary and based off temporary
stimulations—i just wasn't ready. for the being you are. for the
experience you are. for the woman you are. i wasn't ready for the
direction you were heading in, i wasn't ready to hold your hand
and be your eyes when you lost your way, i wasn't ready to be part
of a storyline that i felt i had no place being in. parts of me were
scared of you. scared of the depths that existed within you. scared
of the capacity you had to move ocean waves. my biggest fear was
that my flaws would hinder you from becoming the woman you
need to be. that my own inhibitions would throw rocks on your
path and slow you down from getting to your destination. that
my own shortcomings would become your shortcomings because
pain has a way of being contagious when you're in a connection
with someone who feels as deeply as you do. at the time, i felt i was
being considerate. now, i realize just how selfish i was. distancing
myself from you slowly instead of admitting that i wasn't ready for
you was cowardly, and with hindsight, i can admit that i should've
done better, and that you definitely deserved better.

(continued)

i was still healing.

perhaps, i was attracted to your happiness. the way you managed to make a melodic song every time you opened your mouth to laugh. the way you managed to make the sun envious of your light every time you smiled. the way you managed to speak a fluent language to my insecurities every time you opened your soul. perhaps, because i was so unhappy, i thought that what i needed was someone who could teach me what happiness was. perhaps, because i was so unhappy, i thought that being with someone who had flowers planted in their mind, meant that i could pluck some of those flowers for myself and plant them in my own. perhaps, because i was so unhappy, i just thought that your happiness could rub off on me. how wrong i was, to place my healing in you, and to try to feed off the hard work you had put into yourself. how wrong i was, to fail to realize that happiness is an inside job, and love for myself would be the catalyst for my healing. how wrong i was, for not telling you everything that i was going through, and thinking that all my power laid in being impenetrable, when vulnerability was all our connection ever needed.

i didn't understand love.

what was love? forgive me, but i certainly didn't understand at the time. too many old lovers taught me things about love that were misleading. too many old lovers didn't teach me enough about love, and what it encompasses. too many old lovers claimed to love me but didn't even have love for themselves. so how could i possibly love you in the way you deserve if i didn't even understand what love was? that was a question i needed to ask myself. that was something i needed to have a more intimate conversation with myself about. a one-on-one with my thoughts trying to figure out why i indulged in a connection with you when i didn't understand how to connect with you. and that's what was missing from our love—that deeper understanding. you tried your best to dig beneath my layers, but i didn't make enough of an effort to understand your love language. the past only showed me a surface level of love, but your love language was much louder, more profound, much clearer—but my ears were closed. not on purpose but by habit. i still had much that i had to unlearn from old lovers, but i wasn't honest enough to allow your love to teach me how to love.

gratitude.

when you still feel ill toward someone who hurt you,

you haven't learned your lesson.

be **thankful** they taught you that you deserve better.

(give me all of you, or give me nothing at all)

i no longer fall in love with half-lit **flames** that
have potential to become bigger.

i no longer settle for **semipotent** love.

i want it all.

understand that I do not belong to you;

i was mine long before you came along, and i will continue to
be mine even if you were to go. indulging in a connection isn't a
good enough reason for me to lose all sense of self. indulging in
a connection isn't a good enough reason for me to throw stones
at my wholeness. indulging in a connection isn't a good enough
reason for me to give up my physical and emotional freedom.
subconsciously, you want a love that chains me and tells me
that only you have the right to me. truthfully, i want a love that
encourages me to come up for air, no matter how deep our love
for each other is. i want a love that doesn't require me to ask for
permission to exist. i want a love that doesn't get scared by my
revolutions and doesn't fear my internal liberation. indulging in
a connection only means that i want to share me with you, while
you share you with me. keeping our individual essences alive,
while diluting the idea that for a connection to grow there
needs to be some form of ownership. if love can exist despite
proximity, timing, or situation, my love for you can exist without
attachment. understand that i do not belong to you, and you
do not belong to me.

<u>*honesty.*</u>

i **hope** the words that roll off your tongue
are synonymous with your actions.

i **hope** the intimacy between the two
doesn't require protection.

(you are uniquely you, your journey is uniquely yours, and no one can take that from you)

stop blocking your blessings by comparing your progress to other people. don't look at distractions while the universe is ready to **gift** you. your story is yours—no one else can write it for you. take that pen from their fingertips, and be the protagonist of your own journey. write yourself as you please, paint yourself as you please. you are allowed to exist simultaneously as both **art** and the **artist**.

<u>*spring cleaning.*</u>

thoughts carry weight, memories take up room, and darling,
you have a long journey ahead. sometimes life requires you
to **let go** of the heaviness so you can travel lighter on your journey,
and put the memories on a shelf in the back of your mind
to **create space** for new ones.

realizations:

people's pain doesn't belong to me, and that is something i am **learning**. being a healer also means giving people the space to heal on their own, and that is something i am **learning**.

(she no longer lives at that address you became so familiar with)

that woman you knew yesterday is gone. she exists as a creation
of something much stronger now. she packed her bags
and stopped living in the comfort zone you tried to house her in.
your keys no longer open the doors to her soul.

old connections.

and i had to leave you behind.

not because there was no **love**

but because there was no **growth**.

(the love you want is out there; you're just asking for that love from beings who are incapable of loving you in the way that you deserve. when your passion is matched it will feel like silk, it will feel like honey, it will feel godly. you are magic, darling. never settle)

i **promise** that you're not asking for too much.

i **promise** that you're not being too demanding.

never compromise the intensity of your love.

(my kind of love)

if the love doesn't **electrify** my senses, **illuminate** my soul, fill my dreams with **magic**, and give me **déjà vu** in the morning, i don't want it. i'm worth much more than surface-level love. i'm worth that extra mile, worth that extra effort. worth passionate bones that can hold me up. never settling. match my **passion**, match my **energy**, match my **fire**. otherwise, channel your vibes elsewhere. your love is not meant for me.

divine.

your soul is a place of divinity,

your heart is a sacred temple;

whomever you let enter

should have **clean** feet and **good** intentions.

**selflessness.**

if she prays for you,

keep her **close**.

<u>celebrations.</u>

celebrate the **small** victories, the **quiet** wins, the **silent** achievements. celebrate the magic that happens behind the curtains. clap for yourself even when no one else is watching.

security

let no one silence the **loudness** of your love. if they can't handle
the **intensity** of the music, gently escort them out of the room.

(i'll have two more cups, thanks)

i like my love **strong, sweet,** and **unfiltered**.

**poisonous.**

your healing process will never be identical to anyone else's,

and there is beauty in that. comparison is **poison**, darling.
don't drink that.

<u>**connections and conversations.**</u>

the content of our conversations, the general vibe and flow, tell me so much about our connection. it's hard to swim in **shallow** waters. look at your conversations closely. look at how they leave you feeling after words cease. do you feel **reenergized**, or do you feel **drained**? anyone who doesn't make you feel like magic after you converse shouldn't be given too much energy. treat substance like a staple food.

dead ends.

the end of a connection is not the end of you.

don't walk out of your own life because they walked out on you.

make your way back to yourself, greet yourself with love,

and make a pact with yourself not to let anyone or anything

ever define your worth ever again.

foundations.

we've become so obsessed with the idea of building with
someone that we forget we must lay a **foundation** to grow
first. **communication** is important. **consistency** is important.
vulnerability is important. **honesty** is vital. build your foundation
on solid ground. there's no need to rush. there's no need to force
something into existence. let's swim in each other's waves and get
to know each other first. let's build a foundation so strong that
when tornadoes threaten to engulf us, we can always fall back on
what we've built and find each other again.

imagine.

imagine how much love we would have for ourselves,

if we showed as much desire to find ourselves,

as we show to find other people?

darling,

you're not a burden. your past was never too heavy. their shoulders are just not broad enough to carry a strong woman like you.

when you find her.

when you find her, keep her **close**.

keep her close enough to be **free** when she wants to,

but close enough to let her know you're always there.

love and attachment have nothing to do with each other.

you can love her without being overbearing or imposing.

you can love her **softly**.

she is not a prized possession to be won,

she is not something you put away on a shelf.

she is a woman.

she belongs to herself first.

distance:

if you ever find yourself in a connection where someone continues to take, take, and take, without ever really giving, create **separation**. your soul is not a doormat. your soul is not a landfill for people to dump their baggage. your soul is not a motel for temporary stay. being a good listener is important, but being heard is just as important. don't let empathy and kindness fool you into forgetting your worth.

**much more.**

the first step to healing is acceptance.

stop **romanticizing** people who hurt you.

you've got so much to come.

don't block your blessings.

(more secrets about me)

i had to lose myself to know what **peace** tastes like.

statement:

my silence finds words when speech seems to elude me.

there is no ill intent behind it.

my energy is a **language** that you have to learn.

(forgive them for making you believe that you aren't worthy of love, and forgive yourself for even entertaining the idea that you don't deserve better)

there are parts to you that old lovers couldn't love

that you still hold resentment toward,

because deep down you feel those parts they couldn't love

are the reason why the connection ended.

forgive the people who made you feel unlovable,

but more importantly, **forgive yourself**.

**i hope you do.**

i hope you find **sweetness** in those parts
of you they couldn't love.

i hope you find the **strength** to show those parts
the love they deserve.

<u>*learning me.*</u>

there are parts of me that i didn't know exist, that are still healing. i'm still learning my wounds. i'm learning that healing comes in **stages**. i'm learning that wounds need air to heal. i'm learning to release fear and welcome growth. these wounds will be **flowers** someday. i affirm it.

darling,

many things will make their way back to you, but that doesn't mean that whatever returns is meant to stay. you don't have to make a warm bed for anyone who once left you cold.

impressions.

you're healing, and that terrifies them. they've never met a woman who can break several times and put herself back together using nothing but **self-love**.

(it's simple, really)

love me deeply,

but let me breathe.

drowning me in love won't make me stay.

my love needs **air** to survive.

flow.

you will never need to force what is meant for you.

when the timing is right,

what's yours will open its arms and embrace you tightly.

darling,

lay a red carpet out for your flaws. flourish in your imperfections. show them you have no shame in who you are.

(allow yourself to feel)

your healing process can be **beautiful**. let it be.

(she's one of a kind)

she has the ability to take your breath **away**,

and breathe **life** into you at the same time.

only a woman who talks to **god** can do that.

much rather.

falling in love sounds dangerous.

i'd much rather **grow** in love.

go upward, **water** each other as we go,

build a love that uplifts us both.

we don't have to build a love that is idolized on movie screens.

we can build a love that speaks language only we understand.

a unique love.

a love with no pressure.

a love where we enjoy each other.

a love where we overdose on each other's smiles
and get drunk off our love.

selfishness.

so many temporary people walk around
with some of our deepest secrets.

hold on to your truth like **gold**.

keep some of yourself, to yourself.

darling,

your love is way too deep for someone to only swim halfway for you.

authenticity.

there is beauty in being you, and being accepted and loved for the work of **art** that you are. there is beauty in keeping your aura **authentic**. if i have to change pieces of myself to fit the truth that you wear, then i am doing myself injustice, and doing my growth disservice. we spend so much time and energy trying to keep the smiles on people's faces afloat while we sink into skin that feels so unfamiliar. i promise you, there are people ready to accept you for who you are today. people who have no desire to change you, but to see you **flourish**.

<u>*peace.*</u>

there are people who hurt you who deserve forgiveness.

not because what they did was excusable

but because you deserve **peace** of mind.

(older, and a lot wiser)

i choose **solitude** over forced connections that don't flow.

<u>oxygen:</u>

i distance myself from connections that **suffocate** my soul. i need to be able to come up for **air**. i need to be felt on a **spiritual** level. we need to be growing. we need to be learning from each other. we need to be able to fill spaces with much more than just beautiful noise.

amaranth.

<u>*yours truly.*</u>

there are people still upset with me over things
they did to themselves.

i send my **love**, and **laugh** with the moon about it.

darling,

their exit only made room for amazing people to enter. clean clutter, change the locks on the doors of your soul, keep it moving.

<u>*inner magic.*</u>

i reclaimed my magic when i **stopped** tending to your garden,
and started **watering** my own. i reclaimed my magic
when i started wanting myself more than i wanted you.

darling,

not everyone who promises you love deserves your energy. feel no guilt for caution or selectivity. you don't have to let everyone explore the chapters within you. you can wait for a lover literate enough to read you, and delicate enough to flip the pages in your soul.

<u>*imperfect.*</u>

love is not always beautiful. sometimes love has thorns, **rough** edges, and **sharp** sides. sometimes love has flaws and imperfections. what makes love beautiful is the decision to **choose** love despite how imperfect it is. the decision to choose love through adversity. a love that never gives up is always the best kind of love, and a lover who chooses love is always the best kind of lover.

<u>*unwanted invitations.*</u>

my softness is not an invitation for your recklessness.

my softness does not give you a pass to treat my energy

like a playground for your own enjoyment.

my softness can turn into distance without hesitation.

(thoughts are seeds)

the **key** to manifestation is not believing that whatever
you want is going to come but believing that
whatever you desire is already **yours**.

lessons:

she's still soft. the pain didn't change her heart. the pain didn't change the intensity of her love. the pain only gave her **lessons**.

illusions:

many friends are just acquaintances

who hold some of our deepest secrets.

many friends are strangers

who we share brief exchanges of energy with.

many friends would rather sprinkle sugar

over the truth to try to not upset you.

many friends are **not** friends at all.

patience.

appreciate anyone who sticks around during your healing process.

appreciate anyone who is patient enough to learn your scars.

goddess.

a work of **art**.

her stretch marks remind me that god kissed
her **skin** and wrote poetry on it.

who wouldn't want a woman with **magic** like that?

red herring.

understand that not everyone will want to, or will be able to, meet you halfway, and that's fine. it's a good **omen**. it's a beautiful **sign**. not everyone is meant to meet you halfway, because the universe wants to leave room for someone who actually deserves you, to reach you. lack of reciprocation is never an indication of your worth. your spirit guides are always working in your favor, blocking unneeded energies. let the connection flow, or embrace the lack of waves. everything will happen the way it's supposed to. never force what doesn't make sense.

i promise you, those who are meant to find a way to you, always will. for now, concern yourself with being there for yourself, in **full**.

freedom.

you deserve to **vent** in spaces that don't drown your voice out
when your soul speaks. you deserve to **cry** in spaces that
don't look at your tears as weakness. you deserve to **retreat**
into solitude without your silence being viewed as malicious.
you deserve **judgment-free** connections.

soul cafés

my love is a **full-course** meal.

you have to come with your plate full as well,

if you plan to love me.

(happily ever after)

the beauty in her story is that she didn't wait for anyone
to rescue her. she didn't wait for anyone to sweep her off her feet.
she gave herself the love she knew she deserved, saved herself,
and became the **love of her own life**.

breaking old habits:

i have a tendency to fall for **broken** people. people with pasts that
are **heavy**, people with hearts that have **cracks** in them, people
with experiences that they are still bleeding from. i'm a lover at
heart. a nurturer. a helper. a listener. i have a habit of absorbing
other people's pain, and making it my own. it all happens
subconsciously. i guess the desire to save someone else masks the
fact there are still parts of me that need saving. there are still parts
of me that i need to tend to. there are still parts of me that are
screaming for attention. there are still parts of me that are craving
warmth. being the reason for someone's healing is always lovely,
but being the catalyst for your own **emancipation** is even more
beautiful. therefore, from this day on, i commit to healing. i commit
to self-love. i commit to choosing myself. always, all ways.

<u>*home sweet home.*</u>

i hope you never have to unpack your belongings
in someone else's heart to feel at home.

i hope you return to yourself, and realize that home is **you**.

discoveries.

i have no desire to be with someone who **completes** me.
i'd rather be with someone who shows me there
is more to me than i even knew existed.

<u>*open.*</u>

you gotta love her on a level she can feel you at spiritually.

deep enough for her to dive into,

and open enough for her to come up for air.

(it's time to be reborn. start living again)

stop mourning **versions** of yourself that don't exist anymore.

stop mourning **dead** connections that have no room for growth

—live.

<u>skin deep.</u>

let me undress your mind,

see you emotionally **naked**.

let's make love without touching each other.

let's practice a different kind of **intimacy**.

sacred exchanges:

connections that are filled with effort but don't feel like work. connections that require energy but never leave you on empty. **magic**. effort should never feel draining. exchanging energy should never feel exhausting. separate from anything that separates you from yourself. never feel guilty for distancing yourself from what they want, and gravitating to what you need. self-love is just as **important** as empathy.

<u>transition.</u>

she is no **ordinary** lover.

she was meant to be

experienced differently,

like a transition in

an r&b song or a butterfly

finding its **wings**.

inner glow.

just because you want love from another soul doesn't mean you're ready for it. work on you, do the **inner** work. be ready for what you deserve when it comes. if you feel like you must be in a relationship in order to be happy, then you're not ready for a relationship. don't fool yourself. connections shouldn't be what make or break you. your happiness shouldn't be based on how much or how little someone loves you. sometimes we **attract** souls who can't love us because we haven't learned how to love ourselves. we attract half-lovers because we're half-full. are you ready to be available **unconditionally**? are you ready to be vulnerable? will you choose love even after the honeymoon phase passes? there is beauty and divinity in patience. you are allowed to march to your own tune, and dance to your own beat, unapologetically. don't go chasing things you're not ready for. don't start accepting things you don't deserve.

<u>synergy.</u>

when two givers indulge in a connection, it's like magic.

it's **alchemy**.

i water you, you water me,

we never drain each other, we just **grow**.

love language:

there's a language that your love speaks, that only few will understand. wait for someone who truly matches your heart's **fluency**. someone who listens to beats in your heart and learns your love language, so they can find multiple ways to love you.

a **multilingual** lover.

why settle for vibrations that don't move you? vibrations that don't feel like home? you deserve love that speaks clearly to your soul.

free.

love tastes better when you can **breathe**.

when your lover gives you **oxygen** by letting you be yourself.

(i am not perfect, and i never will be, and i hope you understand that)

i distance myself from people who romanticize perfection. people who fall in love with **illusions**. people who feel i can do no wrong. there may be days when i disappoint you, days when i fall short, days when i can do better, but my heart is always coming from a good place. i need to know you see beyond thorns. i need to know you see beyond parts of me that are hard to touch. i need to know you see the **real** me.

platonic soul mate;

we were not meant to be romantic, we were just meant to be.
although the love we have for each other is undeniable, and
although the love we have for each other exists, it was not meant
to stretch beyond the pure unions of friendship. it was not meant
to stretch at our heart strings, but instead, it was meant to gently
massage them into peace. it was not meant to stretch your legs over
my shoulders at three o'clock in the morning after a night filled
with laughter and conversation. it was not meant to stretch past
the boundaries we subconsciously set to ensure that things don't
become complicated. it was not meant to stretch our connection
into emotional destinations that have no return ticket if we took
that plunge. my love for you is pure. no lust, obligation, or motive
attached to it. so is it so hard to believe that our paths are
perfectly aligned and we were placed in each other's lives even
if it isn't for romantic purpose? is it so hard to fathom that a
deep love can exist between two people whose only intention is
pouring the love that exists between them back into a friendship?
romance is not the only reason the universe brings souls together,
growth and love can exist without it. perhaps we were not
meant to be romantic, perhaps we were just meant to be.

liberation.

i don't want your love

if it comes with **conditions**.

i don't want your love if it **chains** me.

i only want a love that **frees** me.

<u>*hiatus.*</u>

she takes mental **vacations**.

she disappears once in a while to **reclaim** herself.

you need to understand how her energy works.

darling,

you're human. you're allowed to be weak. just don't unpack and live in your sadness. feel it, and move to where there is healing.

a love:

a love that never gives up. a love that finds ways through mazes and roadblocks. a love that always **stays** even when home feels so far away.

a love that never grows old. a love that feels **new** every day. a love that rebirths itself at every moment and baptizes itself in light.

a love that never feels empty. a love that never feels too **full**. a love that you can feel without touch, and touch without feeling.

a love that **grows** you. a love that improves you. a love that manages to kiss your roots with magic and give your petals more color.

a love that evolves. a love that **changes** beautifully. a love that starts rainbows within your soul after every storm, and holds your hand.

(it's time to take off that backpack full of pain)

stop taking pain with you everywhere you go. you deserve to be free from all that **heaviness**. you deserve to travel **lighter** on your journey.

let go of the animosity.

let go of the bitterness.

let go of the resentment.

let go. let go. **let go**.

forgive them, for everything they may have done or may have not done. but more importantly, **forgive yourself**. shed that old skin. be reborn.

amaranth

<u>*questions:*</u>

when was the last time you were kissed by lips that match the symmetry of your soul and held by arms that feel like **home**?

new love.

i don't want to be defined by love you experienced in the **past**.
i want us to define our own love. create our own unique, magical
experience. **unlearn** things past lovers taught you. **learn** new with
me. i promise you, i'll touch and swim in places that old lovers
could never reach.

(the universe has a great sense of humor)

sometimes the universe will let you manifest what you want,

just to show you that you **deserve better**.

seven women i could never forget.

i. it was all about **experiences**. it was a necessity for you to feel. diamonds and gold didn't move you as much as **books** and **flowers**. you liked wine in the morning and coffee in the evening. you liked beethoven when you were happy and trap music when you were sad. your laugh was light, but your mind was heavy. you spent so much time **dreaming**, and not enough time living in the moment.

ii. your eyes were **enchanting**, but the words that came from your lips were even more captivating. gospel to the soul. water to the mind. i remembered every small detail about you, even though you thought it wasn't important. funny thing is, you didn't feel important, you didn't know your **purpose**. if only you knew the power that existed in the little things you said and did. you're a goddess. you'll make a fine mother someday.

iii. you were always a **volcano** waiting to happen, but somehow i was drawn to that. i was drawn to your **passion**, your **spirit**, your **exuberance**. i thought it was beautiful, they felt indifferent. they kept their distance because they thought you were destructive. they didn't understand you, but i did. amid all the confusion, i still chose you, but you chose to push me away. you left burns on my soul and left me picking pieces of myself off the ground. my mother always taught me not to play with fire. i wish i listened.

iv. miss "crystals and sage." miss "zodiac." miss "what is your moon, sun, and rising in?" miss "let me see your chart, so i know it's real." you're appreciated. you taught me so much. your spirituality **fueled** me. your oneness with yourself **inspired** me. your **awareness** opened me, but your overanalyzing closed me. you inadvertently disposed of me. ego killed our connection. can you imagine how far we would've gone if we both just swallowed our pride?

v. my first love. my soul mate. you opened my eyes to things that
i didn't even know existed. you opened my senses to feelings that
i never even knew could be felt. our connection was **intense**, even
though we weren't together for long. but it's hard to write about
you. it's hard to string together sentences and talk about you. a
part of me feels like you don't deserve my words, because you left
without saying a word.

vi. there is so much to you. i have seen the **light** and **dark** sides,
the sun and the moon, but everything is undeniably beautiful.
there was a gentleness about you, even in your rough moments, a
softness about you, even after the way the past treated you. but i
was young, naive, immature. i didn't quite understand what love or
friendship was. i didn't quite understand myself. but you're a good
person, an angel. i hope you found someone who complements
your spirit.

vii. strange. it never moved past friendship, but i'm glad that
it never did. we were always better off as platonic companions.
we mixed together well, without adding romance to the pot. it's
ironic that the reason we don't talk as much anymore is because
we decided not to take that **plunge** into the **unknown**. i miss your
smile, your humor, your friendship. but i also understand that it's
okay to love someone from a distance.

listen:

diluting my truth won't make yours **stronger**.

<u>teachers.</u>

don't let ego block you from acknowledging your blessings. anyone who taught you something about life, or about yourself, was **important**. it's important to take something from every connection. the good, the bad, friends, lovers. it's important to appreciate your teachers. you'll feel a lot lighter once you drop all that bitterness and resentment toward someone. create better memories with new people.

(live to fight another day)

one of the most **beautiful** things you can ever learn is to stop fighting and chasing after people who don't want to stay. no one's absence should ever cause an absence within yourself. you were fine before them, you'll be even better after them.

<u>imagine:</u>

a love that we don't have to define. a love that we don't have to attach a title to. a love that we let **blossom** and just exist.

a love brought together by the love that we have for ourselves already. a love that adds on to the **colorful** pieces we have already.

a love with no pressure. a love that **flows**. a love that only requires you to show up, with no mask or disguises, as yourself.

a love that opens its mouth to profess its existence. a love that never hides. a love that is **immune** to pride and ego.

a love that pours honey on your flaws and scars and shows you how **beautiful** they are. a love that always brings you home.

(understand that not everyone deserves you)

it'll take a certain person to appreciate the beauty in your mind,

and **glow** in your soul, baby.

you can't give everyone pieces of your gold.

darling,

don't you ever get tired of being a home for people who never find their way back? your heart is not a motel for temporary stay.

you fight for them, yet it makes you feel weak. you fight for them, yet you know you need to let go. why are you so scared of freedom?

don't let them carry the key to your happiness in their pocket. change the locks, and ready yourself for a lover who knows how to hold you.

today, tomorrow.

inconsistency is **poison**.

i distance myself from the "here today, gone tomorrow"
kinda people.

my energy is not at your disposal.

(moment of silence)

i had to bury many versions of myself to become the person
i am today, but there are still many versions of me that
deserve funerals, so i can give birth to **peace**.

darling,

how do you expect us to grow, when the conversation doesn't flow?

our line of communication needs to be smooth, sweet, and stimulating. we need to be able to ease over speed bumps and maneuver past roadblocks.

there has to be vulnerability. you need to be able to spill your thoughts to me, and i need to be comfortable enough to do the same.

let's leave ego at the door. meet each other as neutrals. learn you, as you learn me. explore the chapters in each other's souls, slowly.

communication is important. it's food for friendship. it's food for love. if we're not growing, then we're just wasting each other's time.

<u>*evolved.*</u>

i have no desire to be the person i was yesterday.

if you're still hanging on to the person i was, i apologize in advance.

you won't find me.

the woman:

you want the woman who **hears** you when the world tunes you out. the woman who sees you when the world shuts its eyes. a woman full of love.

you want the woman who is **passionate** about herself. the woman who values her inner being. the woman who sees her worth with no mirrors.

you want the woman who is **evolving**. the woman in love with her growth. the woman who doesn't strive for perfection but just wants to be.

<u>false.</u>

the universe has no opinion of you.

the universe only reacts off the energy you give it.

your actions and thoughts are **keys** and **shackles**.

**alone but never lonely.**

you've got to have a certain **divinity** for me to want to share space with you. i'm such an introvert, and i wouldn't have it any other way. being an introvert has given me awareness that only few can understand. i'm thankful for the time alone that i get to learn about myself. you can't connect with other people if you have a disconnect within yourself. nurture your internal relationship. give it **water** and **light**.

darling,

don't stop your blooming process just so they can catch up to you. you've outgrown them for a reason. keep blossoming upward.

remember;

the failure of connections does not dictate your worth. you are not a representation of lovers who could not love you fully.

connections fade away. connections fizzle out. connections end. stop holding yourself accountable for things that were never meant to last.

take the lessons, take the pain, and vibrate higher. trust in the universe's timing. the things that are meant for you, will always stay.

<u>**musical chairs.**</u>

sometimes you only meet your full self later in life.

sometimes you **dance** with the little parts,

until the rest comes out to **hear** the music.

long distance.

some of us are in long-distance relationships with ourselves, and we don't even know it. we give and give and give, pouring energy outward, packing all of our belongings, resting in others' hearts, while abandoning home. if your heart could speak, would it shed tears of **happiness**, or tears of **pain**? would it speak of its fullness, or reveal secrets of neglect? the relationship you have with yourself is important. don't look to **decorate** others' hearts while your soul is in need of spring cleaning. you are deserving of the warmth you radiate within others. you are deserving of the love you give to other people. you are deserving.

<u>*to the woman.*</u>

to the woman who isn't celebrated: i hope you're applauding yourself every day for how beautiful you are, even without their validation.

to the woman with a broken heart: i hope you're filling the cracks with love and patience. i hope your healing is starting to taste sweet.

to the hopeless romantic woman: i hope your love is still as strong as whiskey, and still as gentle as silk. i hope pain hasn't softened your love.

(places you'll never find me)

you'll never find me where my energy isn't appreciated.

you'll never find me planting my **roots** in places that
don't support my growth.

i hope you do.

i hope you find a lover who starves their **ego** and **feeds** their love for you. a lover who loves unashamedly and allows you to love yourself.

i hope you find a lover who lets you **exist**. a lover who loves you but lets you be. a lover who keeps you close but allows you to **breathe**.

i hope you find a lover who finds **joy** in your being. a lover who **celebrates** your existence. a lover who speaks to god about you.

parts of me.

parts of me are still learning. i feel things so **deeply**. i can take so much from a connection that had very little, and carry parts of connections that should be released. much of it has to do with the fact that i pour large quantities of myself into everything i indulge in. i cannot dilute my emotions. i cannot half feel anything. i cannot fake the vibe. i can only give every part of me, in all its entirety, in all its **rawness**, in all its **nakedness, unhidden**. parts of me are still learning that some people are temporary, and should remain temporary. parts of me are still learning that it's okay to let go of people who are no longer conducive to my journey. parts of me are still learning that my love deserves intensity and fire that matches my own. parts of me are still learning.

darling,

spend less time explaining yourself and spend more time swimming in your truth. your mind and energy are not for everyone.

<u>*depth.*</u>

love from a woman who's in love with herself is **deep**.

there's something **godly** about a woman who can give,

without taking away from herself.

(they misunderstand my reclusiveness, but i understand it fully)

solitude taught me self-love.

<u>labor.</u>

i've worked too hard on my happiness,

to be affected by people and things that don't understand

the **energy** and **time** i've put into myself.

<u>stages and phases.</u>

at a stage in my life where **consistency** is more important than **intensity**. i'd rather know your energy is true even at its lowest.

at a stage in my life where growth is a **staple food**. i need to be growing, progressing, shifting. i need to be better than i was yesterday.

at a stage in my life where i will never sacrifice **peace** of mind for love, companionship, or friendship. my peace is **guarded** by self-love.

at a stage in my life where the past no longer has **power** over me. i've forgiven, and forgiven myself. i no longer carry **guilt** in a backpack.

at a stage in my life where **happiness** is always the choice. my thoughts shape everything around me. sadness will not build a home inside me.

woman,

your mind is a sanctuary full of light and roses that deserves to be worshipped just as much as your body.

<u>*comfort zones.*</u>

love can never really grow if it makes comfort zone a **home**.

there will be times when love requires you to **shed** old skin
and embody something new. you can re-create
your love as many times as you need.

the right lover will never make you feel like you're
doing too much or doing too little. the energy will just **flow**.

love can only exist where **vulnerability** exists.
love can only exist where **honesty** exists.
love can only exist where judgment doesn't exist.

projections.

never let anyone **project** their insecurities on you. that's a lot of heaviness to carry around. you don't deserve all that unnecessary **weight**.

learn the difference between being a **healer**, and being **baggage** for people's emotional weight. discernment is so important.

your mental health is everything. **peace** of mind is everything. don't sacrifice any of that to save someone's soul. you need yourself too.

mikado.

(show up for yourself)

learn to be **present** in other people's lives,

without becoming **absent** in your own.

forgiveness.

you can forgive someone and still want absolutely nothing to do with them. you can create distance from someone with no resentment attached. love and attachment have nothing to do with each other. i can love you just as intensely from a distance. there's no mileage on my love. some connections require space to survive. some need to die in order to be reborn. some connections need to be released for you to breathe.

the show must go on

who were you before they broke you?

stop holding on to whoever that person was

—they're gone now.

stop injecting yourself with nostalgia

and overdosing on the memories.

after all their actions you're still here.

beautiful, resilient, healing, a masterpiece.

applaud yourself.

darling,

your growth is too important for you to drop your standards for someone who can't meet you at the level you deserve to be met at. trust the alignment or misalignment of your connections. if you're sacrificing more than you're receiving, that connection isn't for you. some people will never be ready when you're ready, but you're not obliged to wait for them. you'll be met halfway by those who deserve you.

<u>riding the waves.</u>

it's okay to feel.

dive into what you're feeling.

soak in the emotions.

absorb the lessons.

just don't swim in the waves for too long.

**gold.**

she's made out of **affirmations** and self-love.

you can't **break** a woman like that.

a letter to the person i was;

i understand why you moved through life the way you did. why you navigated through the waves like a ship on the brink of sinking. why you tiptoed across paths like there was hot charcoal beneath your feet. i understand why you felt as if the way you moved would dictate the way others moved around you. you thought you understood self-love—how naive you were. to think that self-love was a thing that you just mastered overnight. to think that self-love was something as simple as uttering the words "i love myself." but self-love is much deeper than that. much more intricate. self-love is a journey that requires you to show up, in your fullest entirety, naked, open, flawed. every day requires you to be available for yourself, because some days no one else will be available for you. so instead of seeking so much outward, seek more within yourself. there's a gold mine that exists within you, that only you can reach—never let anyone dig that out. you'll slip up on some days, and you'll forget how smooth it feels to soak in self-love, but take time learning how to love yourself—this isn't a race.

**sweet solitude.**

don't take my solitude personally.

at times it tastes **sweet** being alone.

at times **applauding** myself feels better
than attention from crowds.

<u>**self-love nonchalance.**</u>

never apologize to anyone for wanting yourself more.

only apologize to yourself for not realizing earlier
that you were all you ever needed.

<u>*heartache:*</u>

i have no bitterness in my bones. but heartache has been one of my greatest teachers. i'm a lot wiser, a lot more understanding, a lot more aware. my forgiveness does not have any attachment associated with it. forgiveness is a commitment to myself. that even though i have let go of how someone made me feel, i will honor my needs too. i will honor my well-being too. i will honor my peace of mind too. i can forgive you, and want absolutely nothing to do with you, and if it serves to help me flourish, blossom, and grow, then there is absolutely nothing wrong with that.

(you are responsible for your healing)

there are people who make evenings feel like 9 a.m., and turn wounds into testimonies. they're not responsible for your healing— you are.

we have a habit of looking outward for healing. thinking that the tools to mend our souls are in others' possession, when we hold the keys.

spend time with yourself. take your wounds on a date and understand them better. your healing lies in how honest you can be with yourself.

**quiet flowers.**

the strongest ones bleed in silence.

have no one applauding their growth.

have no one watching their healing process.

they **bloom in silence**.

darling,

perhaps the reason you've been attracting conditional lovers is because you haven't been unconditionally loving yourself. you set the tone for how people love you. love for yourself will show them how you desire and deserve to be loved.

**communication.**

more **honest** conversations with yourself.

more **vulnerable** conversations with yourself.

more conversations with your, self.

(speak it into existence)

a lover who doesn't try to **calm** the oceans inside of you. a lover who knows how to swim in the waves you give off.

a lover who tries to understand your love language. a lover who never gets tongue-tied when **expressing** their feelings for you.

a lover who never hides. a lover with **passion** you never have to question. a lover who always meets you halfway, regardless of the journey.

affirmation;

i will no longer carry people's guilt in my back pocket. i will not take responsibility for people's insecurities. i am free.

<u>old literature.</u>

there are poems inside you,

that belong to your parents,

old friends,

and ex-lovers.

don't carry around old chapters.

write yourself anew.

__battleground.__

a healing woman will have flowers
blooming from the cracks in her heart.

her inner **aura** will resemble a
battleground filled with hope.

(where there is no depth, i fail to exist)

if your definition of love is too shallow for me to dive into,

i'd rather find somewhere else to swim.

darling,

you've got magic in your bones, and gold in your soul. don't let anyone treat you like you're ordinary.

choose yourself:

i hope you learn that choosing yourself will always be the most beautiful love language you can ever learn. i hope you prioritize yourself. i hope you learn never to betray your intuition. i hope you learn to open your soul and listen when god is speaking to you. i hope you learn to grow from past inflictions. i hope you stop using the past as an excuse for stagnancy and realize your divinity.

safe returns.

i had to step away from a few,

and walk back into my own life,

to realize how much i had missed myself.

to the woman with an old soul;

your way of thinking is appreciated. your way of feeling is appreciated. your way of being is appreciated. don't let them whisper lies in your ears—the way your mind works is not outdated, it's beautiful. your undying wisdom of the world and the way it dances, your appreciation for art and literature, your hopeless romanticism and faith in the concept of love, darling, you're walking poetry, and you don't even know it. your rib cage is made out of piano keys, your heart is a drum, and they make a unique melody that only few will understand. they tell stories of a woman who has seen so much, felt so much, been so much, evolved, but still moves to her own rhythm. whether life forced you to grow up too fast, or you're carrying on from where you left off in a previous lifetime, to the woman with an old soul, you're beautiful, and you're appreciated.

promises.

i promise you;

you are worthy of love just as you are. you don't have to change anything about yourself to receive the love you deserve.

i promise you;

you are enough just as you are. you don't have to live trying to prove yourself to people committed to misunderstanding you.

i promise you;

you are deserving of peace just as you are. you don't have to break pieces of yourself in order to keep other people whole.

(it always will)

the best kind of love will always find you.

you will **never** have to go looking for it.

__regardless.__

what i like about her is that she **blooms**
whether you water her or not.

whether you give her **light** or not.

she **exists** without your existence.

<u>*courage.*</u>

i've been learning recently that it takes a lot of courage to be honest with yourself. to take sips of the truth no matter how bitter it may taste, or how uncomfortable it may feel. to dive into the truth no matter how violent the waves may be, or how deep it may appear. to look the truth deep in the eyes no matter how daunting it may be, or how scary it may seem. of course, the people you love deserve authenticity, the people you care about deserve sincerity, but you are deserving as well. you are deserving of the honesty you give others. you are deserving of the peace that comes with the truth. but sometimes that peace only comes when you confront those inner demons that you've been hiding from for so long. when you stop focusing on the honesty others deserve, and start focusing on the honesty you and your inner child deserve. it's easier to tell others the truth, and harder to be truthful with yourself. i've been learning recently that it takes a lot of courage to be honest with yourself.

(they are not for you)

some will be intimidated by how deeply you love yourself.

you are not obligated to shallow your depth
or tame your intensity for them.

intentions.

sometimes the most powerful intentions are silent. ones where you don't have to say a thing. ones where your actions reveal where you stand. words aren't always necessary. sometimes the way you water yourself and treat yourself, will show them how you deserve to be received. don't preach to deaf ears. save your words for those willing to learn your love language. leave room for those who are meant to reach you.

wasted ink.

i no longer write apology letters to parts of myself
that no one accepted.

i just show those parts **love** and **celebrate** them even more.

burdens.

your wounds will never be a burden to a lover who has ears that never close and has **patience** that runs deeper than oceans.

your wounds will never be a burden to a lover who **appreciates** your journey so far, and pours honey on parts of you that still need healing.

your wounds will never be a burden to a lover who **celebrates** your being by the sun, and thanks god for your existence with the moon.

(stay away from me unless you plan to decorate my mental space)

falling deeply in love with myself,

and unless you plan to add depth to the oceans i swim in already,

keep your distance and stay at shore.

darling,

you've spent too much time and energy on your knees begging
them not to leave, when love for yourself is the only love you
should be fighting for to stay.

(you deserve patience)

anyone rushing your growth,

or anyone impatient with your healing process,

doesn't deserve any part of you when you've fully bloomed.

darling,

you will heal. it may not be today, tomorrow, or the day after, but you will heal. take your sweet time; this is not a race.

_i am._

i am rough around the edges.

i am imperfect in my thought process.

i am a work in progress.

but i am worthy of love and all its sweetness.

(you are not an apology letter, darling. don't live like one)

stop apologizing for the days when you
don't have the strength to smile.

the days when silence speaks better for you.

swim in your truth.

(never too much)

love yourself enough,

that people's departures don't feel like funerals,

and their absences are the **catalyst** to love yourself even harder.

magic show.

your healing doesn't have to be loud, apparent, and beautiful.

it's not a magic show the world needs to see—
it's magic that happens within.

(don't change your essence to suit mine)

you've got to **excite** me and give me life.

you've got to fill my **lungs** with air and make my **heart** feel warm.

but you have to come as you are.

<u>*short-term memory.*</u>

don't get so wrapped up in other people's journeys that you forget that your path deserves unique **footprints** of its own. don't get so absorbed in other people's stories that you forget that you are a vast book with empty pages waiting to be **written**.

(things I have learned over the years)

consistency is **food** to a woman's soul.

as we are.

changing me to fit your idea of love won't work.

changing yourself to fit my idea of love

won't work. let's create our own kind of love.

awaken.

stop waiting for an apology from the people who hurt you
to finally give yourself permission to heal. make love
to the parts of yourself that old connections disconnected.
dip the parts they broke in self-love. wait for no one
to come along and kiss your wounds.

right lovers.

the right lover will never cause anxiety.

you will feel at peace.

they will **cease the wars** in your chest and
fill your bones with nectar.

an ode to a future lover;

understand that i am not perfect. i am a work in progress. there are things past lovers taught me that i am trying to unlearn, and things past lovers never taught me that i am trying to learn. there are oceans within me that are too deep to swim in on some days, and roads within me that are not always easy to travel on. there are love languages that are still foreign to me, and there are chapters in my soul that are hard to digest. i practice self-love like children perfecting their melodies on guitar strings, and sometimes that can be misunderstood. my love for you will never overshadow the love i should have for myself, and i hope you understand that. i have drowned myself too many times trying to save other people in the name of love, and i will no longer steer my boat into rivers that don't help me float. i hope you love yourself enough to understand that you deserve the same. i hope you love me enough to let me love myself. i require patience. i require open ears. i require vulnerability, but above all, i require you to understand that i am not perfect. i am a work in progress.

woman,

some will be confused by how loyal you are to yourself. how loyal
you remain to your truth. don't pluck your roots to be understood.

<u>love languages.</u>

make her **playlists** and send her **books**.

feed her soul and water her mind.

serenade her intellect,

and **communicate** with her on a deeper level.

fatal attraction.

i look at some of the things and people i used to put up with, and
i realize that i was only attracting mirrors within me i had to
heal from. ego can be poison. it's easy to victimize yourself while
pointing the finger at other people for how your own energy looks
in the mirror. take accountability of the things you attract.

(don't give up on her so soon)

she's **learning** to love herself.

it can be an internal war on some days

and it can be bliss on others.

through it all, she deserves **patience**.

to my future son;

softness isn't a weakness. being impenetrable doesn't make you strong. there's life in being unapologetically vulnerable.

**illusionary homes.**

are you loving a comfort zone, or are you loving someone who encourages you to explore places of yourself that make you uncomfortable so you can grow from the darkness? not everyone who provides you with warmth is good for your growth.

(don't leave god unread)

god speaks to you through your **intuition**.

your intuition speaks to you in the way people make you **feel**.

don't leave internal messages **unread**.

to the hopeless romantic woman;

i love how full of love you are. i love how full of warmth you are. i love how your love cup overflows and leaves leftovers after breakfast and dinner. i love how you carry the sun in your chest and the moon in your lungs, and how every time you move and breathe, your magic is felt regardless of the time of day. it's not your fault they can't meet you halfway. it's not your fault they're unwilling to bend so that their heart can fit the symmetry of yours. it's not your fault they can't grasp the essence of the magical being you are. there's no such thing as having too much love, or loving too hard, so darling, let's dispel that myth. you are perfect the way you are. full of light, full of imagination, full of love. don't change yourself to attract a lover who feels good on the surface but can't comprehend your love language. don't dial down the intensity of your love so you are lukewarm enough to hold for someone who can't handle a real woman. maybe you aren't hopeless after all. maybe you're just a romantic who has yet to find her equal, and until that person comes along, keep love for yourself burning strong, and keep your love light on.

(don't interrupt her)

and when you see her glowing,

dripping gold from her pores,

turning wounds into flowers,

loving herself unconditionally—**let her be**.

beautiful impatience.

i no longer give toxic people patience.

i no longer give their toxicity room to breathe.

i no longer try to make their poison taste sweet.

more unpaid debts.

you don't owe temporary people **loyalty**.

people who have no intention of staying and choosing **love**.

you owe yourself the love you gave them.

still.

and here you are after all the pain and heartbreak,

still **soft,**

still **loving,**

still **hopeful,**

still **magical,**

still **whole,**

still **beautiful.**

<u>*hindsight.*</u>

you felt warm at first; you looked like love up close.

but what you were was a lesson disguised as love,

a lesson on how to love myself.

i said goodbye to you a long time ago;

no words were exchanged, but i let you out of the doors to my soul silently. i didn't force you out, i just eased you out, day by day, until i couldn't feel your presence anymore. i remember all the times burning while trying to save the home i built in your heart. i remember all the times when i found myself drowning in violent waves trying to save the shipwreck of a connection that we had. i remember looking around waving for help and being the only one fighting. i remember being the only one trying to gather what fell off, so i could rebuild the broken pieces of what we had. but that was all an illusion. i woke up one day and i realized that i was fighting a battle that was meant to be fought by two people, alone. i realized that the only person i was battling was myself. closure is a funny thing. we often misinterpret words as a means of closure, but your silence and your actions were all the closure i ever needed. so now, when you text my phone and i leave you unread, or you call me and i don't pick up, you shouldn't be surprised. i said goodbye to you a long time ago.

darling,

you'll lose your mind trying to be for everyone. your soul's coated in honey. some don't like the taste of sugar, and that's fine.

gratitude, gratitude:

my heart no longer skips beats when i think of you.

instead, i'm overcome with a beautiful peace and tranquility,

when i realize just how much space your departure

created for beautiful things to enter my life.

to whom this may concern;

thank you for giving up on me. thank you for being a teacher.
thank you for giving me fuel to love myself harder.

analog girl,

you weren't made for this digital world. you're far too full of wonder and far too full of depth to let them minimize your worth through a screen. you've got too much magic in your mind to entertain lovers who have to google search answers to meet you at your level. when's the last time you had a face-to-face conversation? the last time you looked someone deeply in the eyes, and they took a selfie of your soul? not a digital one but a mental one. one they carry with them everywhere they go. one that shows how brightly your soul smiles when it rains and reminds them how full of love you are? when's the last time you put your phone away, stripped your mind down, and let someone massage your senses? when's the last time your connections were based on how much you knew someone away from the short messages and misconstrued texts? when's the last time someone really took your soul out for a date and fed you mentally? you get lost in this digital world sometimes, but i know you crave something a lot deeper. something a lot more meaningful. something with a lot more substance. some may call you old-fashioned, but i think it's beautiful. how connected you are to a period in time when connections and mindsets really meant something. when connections weren't based on how much we text a day, and when the last time we facetimed was. when connections were all about time spent, and experiences felt. analog girl, you weren't made for this digital world.

darling,

it's never too late to live life unapologetically. you can blossom freely without worrying about what they think of your petals.

___discoveries.___

warm light from her eyes,

melodies on her skin.

she's not glowing because she found another soul,

she's glowing because she found herself.

viridian.

<u>**unexpected returns.**</u>

when they walk away, let them.

open the door, let them free.

but if they come back,

understand you're not obligated to open that door again.

**masks.**

i'd rather you be real than hidden.

i'd rather you be honest than sympathetic.

i'd rather you be true than apologetic.

be **undisguised**.

<u>*self-worth.*</u>

a woman who knows her worth is a beacon.

she's god in human form.

she's embodiment of love.

you can't give her half a lung, she's worth life.

a woman who knows her worth
requires you to know your worth as well.

the gold in her soul has to be a reflection
of gold that exists in you.

a woman who knows her worth will never be easy.

she's free from attachment, she's full of love.

she doesn't need your attention to exist.

(speak it into existence)

i hope you find a lover whose only demand
is that you continue to soak in self-love,

while you sculpt yourself into the masterpiece you are.

i hope you find a lover who lets you breathe.

a lover who allows you space to reclaim yourself,
and never views your silence as malicious.

i hope you find a lover whose love for themselves
improves the love you have for each other.

a lover who adds color onto your soul's canvas.

(find worth in yourself first)

don't come looking for me until you've found yourself.

don't come looking for me until you've found your **inner god**.

my love.

my love is way too **loud** to be confined under covers.

my love is way too **bright** to be hidden in dark rooms.

my love cup **overflows**.

darling,

stop settling and wait for what you deserve. aren't you tired of breathing life into people who don't keep your flame burning? you're only comfortable settling because subconsciously, you don't believe that you deserve better. detox from that opinion. renew yourself. the love you want is out there. entertaining surface-level love blocks the path for the right lover to reach you. wait for what you deserve.

renovation.

and when you finally decide to close the door

that's been open to them for so long,

feel no guilt for changing the locks

and only allowing the ones with intentions of staying to come in.

i value peace more than fascination;

i value peace more than intrigue. i value peace more than
fireworks. "getting butterflies" doesn't appeal to me as much as
having calm, relaxing energy over me. getting butterflies doesn't
appeal to me as much as having someone who caresses your rib
cage gently and ensures your heart drum beats consistently. getting
butterflies doesn't appeal to me as much as meeting someone who
manages to swim in the waves i give off, instead of unbalancing
the waves within me. the novelty has never appealed to me. i don't
want a lover who makes me feel uneasy or anxious when we touch.
i don't want a lover who causes my mind to run in circles when i
think about how many hours it's been since we last spoke. i don't
want a lover who causes my soul unrest when i reminisce about our
last night under the stars. i want a lover who fills me with ease,
fills me with sweetness, fills me with soothing melodies. i want
a lover who feels like home and not an amusement park. i want a
lover who smooths my rough edges and doesn't leave me on edge.
i want a lover who massages my soul after our interactions and
leaves me feeling like silk. i want a lover who fills me with peace,
because i value peace more than fascination.

eternity.

she's a woman with a mind that leaves
french kisses on your soul.

she's the kind of woman you only have
to feel once to remember forever.

__understand.__

understand that there are people who will taste good but won't fill your soul up. people who only bring half of themselves to the table.

understand that there are people who'll find you beautiful but be so mesmerized by the surface that they overlook the flowers in your soul.

understand that there are people who will want to change your soul's makeup because they can't appreciate your internal revolutions.

understand that there are people who will applaud your healing in person but secretly hope that you never evolve past their comfort zone.

understand that people's intentions will not always match their actions, but you don't owe your loyalty to anyone who doesn't value your energy.

darling,

the more you pour into yourself, the more ways you find back to yourself. self-love is the map that brings you back home.

<u>**bridges.**</u>

she was misunderstood,

she didn't **burn** bridges.

she simply destroyed the path for anyone
who didn't deserve her energy to reach her.

when you fall.

and when you fall, i pray you fall into arms that are firm but still feel soft, arms that are ready to sustain pressure, arms that feel safe.

and when you fall i pray it doesn't feel like falling at all. i pray it feels like ascension. i pray you grow wings and fly to new heights.

and when you fall i pray you allow yourself to experience this love differently. i pray you don't let the past stop you from feeling fully.

little, big lies.

your insecurities are liars; silence them, don't listen to them.

you are worthy of **love** and worthy of **forgiveness**.

you are worthy of everything that you desire.

butterfly effect.

i am always finding myself. i am never a finished article. on some days i am **healed,** and on others i am still **healing**. on some days i'm a **pen**, and on other days i'm a **journal**. i am always evolving.

<u>clarity.</u>

when i realized that i was whole alone,

i stopped entertaining people who only gave me half of themselves.

perspective:

the funny thing about us is that we like to take accountability
for the good things we attract, but when we attract undesirable
things or situations, we try to shift the blame on others for our
pain. the universe doesn't work like that. take accountability for
everything you attract. everything you attract is a manifestation of
something that exists within you. something that you've thought,
experienced, spoke, or something buried deep inside you that you
may not have addressed yet. the key is not to look at anything you
manifest as good or bad but to look at everything you attract as a
lesson. a puzzle piece needed to complete the overall picture. a lock
combination needed to unlock your healing and emancipation.

(questions)

she knows what love looks like because she is love.

how could you possibly give a woman
like that less than what she is?

(more secrets about me)

when the flame i had for you stops burning, it's hard
to reignite me again. it's hard to refuel my passion,
it's hard to rekindle my enthusiasm. it's hard for me
to exist in spaces that no longer have oxygen.

<u>impenetrable.</u>

the **softest** people i know,

are the **strongest** people i know.

they have stories that could've broken them,

but they manage to take all of those pieces and reinvent themselves.

spontaneity

no cliché good-morning texts. send her affirmations
to get her day started. talk to god about her for a few minutes.
feed her soul with light, and plant flowers in her mind.
remind her of her undying divinity.

<u>lost letters.</u>

to whom this may concern;

you've lived for other people for too long. dedicated so much
energy into ensuring their smiles don't fade away while you
destruct quietly. it's time to pour back into you. it's time to
reclaim yourself.

to whom this may concern;

stop running away from yourself, and start confronting your fears.
you deserve truth, you deserve clarity, you deserve peace. come
back to yourself, your soul deserves a home-cooked meal.

to whom this may concern;

in case no one has ever told you, i'm proud of you. look at the
strides you've taken. look at how you've stripped yourself of guilt
and people's judgment. you're living, love. you're living in self-love.

loud.

silent love was never meant for me. i like the kind of love i can hear through the speakers in my soul. the kind of love that has **bass** that gently vibrates in my bones. love i can feel without touching.

(the older version of me doesn't exist anymore)

you don't recognize me anymore, and i'm glad. you try to find versions of me that expired, but they no longer exist. while you were stuck on the person i was, **i evolved, i recognized, i grew**. i'm just more in love with myself these days.

just be.

stop putting timelines and deadlines on your healing, and just be.

be kind to yourself, be patient with your process.

be a little selfish with your energy, and **drink cups of self-love** unapologetically.

woman;

treat yourself the way you would treat your daughter. with
love, with softness, with patience. treat yourself in a way that
encourages you not to look outward but to constantly admire the
gold that exists within you already.

(i am many things)

i am many **unfinished** poems.

i am many **unwritten** love songs.

i am many **unplayed** melodies.

i am many things people can't appreciate or understand,

and that's why i make the effort to understand
the flowers blooming within myself.

darling,

the way people leave you, the way they exit your life, the way they leave their relationship or connection with you is all the closure you need. find clarity in actions, not words.

(close your ears)

let no one tell you how to wear your feelings. don't let them
tell you what colors don't look good on your soul. don't let them
tell you when to cover your heart or leave it naked.
feel whatever you feel, whenever you feel, with no guilt.

shell.

be **protective** of you. your aura. be protective of the garden that
you've watered for so long within you. you've worked too hard on
yourself to let anyone with dirty feet walk all over your soul.

darling,

when will you stop letting the mirror tell you how beautiful you are and start recognizing the magic that exists in your bones? you are more than your vessel. you are stories, experiences, and poems all in one. you are love.

<u>*returning home.*</u>

if my love doesn't stay, that doesn't mean there wasn't any love at all. if i'm all about me now, that doesn't mean i was never all about you. i'm pouring what i poured into you, back into **me**.

(wild in the most gentle way)

they are scared of women like you. women with hearts big enough to house suitcases full of **pain**. women with laughs so therapeutic they can heal **wounds**. women with passion fierce enough to start **wildfires**. they are scared of what they can't tame or understand.

<u>*small steps.*</u>

never let sadness build a home inside of you.
allow its unexpected visits, learn from it while it's there,
but then open the door and slowly let it out.
sadness deserves no permanent resting place in your heart.

lost letter to an old friend.

there are parts to me that don't exist anymore, parts to me i left behind years ago, parts to me i left behind moments ago. i'm constantly shedding, and constantly growing new skin, because i'm trying to evolve past the things that don't stimulate me anymore, past the things that don't speak to me anymore, past the things that don't fill me anymore. and if i left you behind during my process, understand that it wasn't out of malice, it wasn't out of selfishness, it wasn't out of egotism. it was out of self-love, and i hope even you can appreciate that.

lost letter to my old self.

it's never too late to be everything that you wanted. it's never too late to live the life that you've always envisioned. it's never too late to commit to something that you feel will serve you well going forward. but you have to drop that fear. you have to drop that doubt. you have to drop all of that poison, and start feeding yourself things that improve you. you have to let go of all of those inhibitions that have stopped your feet from moving and clipped your wings. you have to start living in your truth.

lost letter to an ex-lover.

i don't hate you. quite the opposite. i'm actually quite thankful for you. thankful for all the lessons you taught me, and thankful for all the things you never showed me. it's funny how the same things that break you, can be the same things that liberate you. it's crazy how the same things that hurt you, can be the same things that emancipate you. in a strange way, you saved me. your lack of love helped me see the lack of love i had for myself. it made me realize just how much i lost myself in you, and how much i wanted myself back. so, thank you.

(you are not responsible for someone else's insecurities)

it is not your responsibility to babysit people's insecurities. you are not obligated to slow down your bloom so they can meet you at a level they are comfortable with. your growth is too important to dim the light within you for someone still trying to find their own.

never.

i have no interest in being for everyone.

sometimes my truth will taste like **whiskey**,

and sometimes my truth will taste like **nectar**,

but i will never dilute myself for anyone.

darling,

this healing comes in **waves**. on some days you will drown, and on other days you will float. on some days you will feel broken, and on other days you will feel renewed. be patient with yourself.

new beginnings.

when your soul feels heavy, unpack. take that bag off and take a closer look inside. why are you still holding on to situations that weigh you down? why are you still fighting for connections that disconnect you? get rid of what no longer serves you. you deserve to feel lighter.

<u>unrequited.</u>

when their love for you doesn't have a voice,

awaken the voice inside of yourself.

let the love you have for yourself speak for you.

let your love for yourself be so loud,

that it fills their silence with beautiful **music**.

(thank you)

my growth comes with no apology letter attached to it.

it comes with no honey-coated words and actions.

it comes with no guilt or regret.

i'm **grateful** for anyone i left behind,

because your absence helped me find more of myself.

(do your future lover a favor)

the most beautiful thing you can do for your future lover,

is learning how to love yourself before you meet them.

to whom this may concern;

i have not forgotten about us. i have just remembered how much more i need, me. i have remembered how warm it is to wrap myself in solitude, and how sweet self-love tastes. i have remembered how beautiful it is to return home to myself.

darling,

you are not a shelter for people's pain, you are not a cure for people's loneliness, you do not live to validate anyone. it is not your job to breathe life into people's existence and decorate anyone's comfort zone.

accountability.

hold your friends and family accountable when they hurt you. hold yourself accountable when you hurt them. **disguising energy** and **camouflaging truth**, does not make pain and wounds disappear.

exchanges.

dialogue is **oxygen**, conversations are energy,

words are **food**.

your soul is too vast to be feeding on anything that doesn't fill you.

you deserve exchanges that feel like full-course meals.

broken mirrors.

i am aware of my magic,

and too aware of my own magic,

to entertain anyone who is not aware of their own.

<u>undercover.</u>

a woman's silence is not an absence of love.

a woman's silence is not an overflux of emotion.

a woman's silence can be energy and intention
that speak more fluently for her than words.

selfless woman;

you ever get tired of breathing life into people who fill your lungs with poison? you ever get tired of massaging people's egos with your tongue? it is not selfish to want more of you than them.

healing woman;

who taught you that pain should be hidden? who taught you to label your scars with shame? unlearn what you learned. your wounds deserve honesty. your wounds deserve air. you deserve peace.

reserved woman;

there is power in knowing when silence speaks better for you. there is magic in knowing who is for you and who isn't. there is beauty in being able to blossom on your own. feel no guilt for being cautious of how you receive or give out your energy.

<u>emancipation.</u>

realizing that i'm not for everyone,

was the most beautiful thing i ever learned.

realizing that i'm not for everyone,

emancipated me and took the handcuffs off my spirit.

(one of a kind)

some women wait for applause.

women like her **celebrate themselves**.

darling,

be wary of the souls that belittle your growth. the ones intimidated by your happiness. the ones who envy the intensity of your smile. sharing laughter with a few people does not turn them into friends or lovers.

differences.

there's a difference between being difficult to love and being with someone who isn't patient enough to learn you and your love language. remember that.

<u>listening ears.</u>

the right lover will never try to silence your wounds
when they become too loud.

their soul will **open** its ears,

listen to what they have to say,

and gently caress you into a space of peace.

(you carry the keys to your emancipation)

don't let empathy force you into staying in spaces
that poison your spirit,

and drag your soul in the mud.

you can leave whenever you want to.

goodbyes can taste bitter in the moment,
but the aftertaste can be so **sweet**.

<u>assumptions.</u>

you don't need to be what people assume you to be.

you'll break your back carrying around
illusions people have attached to you.

don't let people clothe you in ideas
and opinions that don't **fit your soul**.

new acquaintances.

i had to leave my old self behind,

so i could meet who i needed to be.

<u>testimonies.</u>

women like you don't exist by mistake.

women like you are walking scriptures.

you could let heartache harden you,

but you remain **soft** anyway,

and that's a **testimony** in itself.

losing your love was the best thing to ever happen to me;

the day we went our separate ways, it felt like a funeral. your words hit me across the head and your actions buried my soul six feet under. but the truth is, i dug my own grave. i continuously served you full platters of love, feeding your soul for breakfast, lunch, and dinner, while i went to sleep hungry and woke up empty. i lost a sense of me, when one of the only things a connection should do is strengthen your sense of self. while others may shift the blame to the other person in the connection, claiming that perhaps "they never loved them correctly," i take full responsibility for not loving myself correctly. not loving myself with the same intensity i loved you with. not loving myself with the same passion i loved you with. not loving myself with the same enthusiasm i loved you with. but losing you gave me perspective. in a strange way, maybe a funeral is symbolic of burying the old me and birthing something new. losing your love was the best thing to ever happen to me because it gave me the opportunity to find love for myself.

<u>**beautiful enigma.**</u>

sometimes she has it all together, and sometimes
she's in the process of re-creating herself. she's fought
so many wars internally, and you don't understand
her battles enough to tell her how to **color** her emotions.

darling,

while you're praying for someone who mistreats you to change their behavior, you are someone else's prayer. shift your energy from those you know don't deserve you. wish them well, thank them for the lessons, and unpack your soul in spaces that celebrate you.

(when the music stops)

i no longer **dance** in spaces that have the desire to change the
music every time they can't handle the rhythm of my progression.
my growth may intimidate some, but i will not put stop signs along
my journey to caress egos and maintain temporary connections.

future lover;

i'm not meant to be a home for you. build a home in yourself so you never feel alone when i'm not around. plant affirmations and seeds of love in your soul so we can both grow, but understand that attachment will only shallow the depth of our love.

**oceans.**

self-love is the only ocean you can never **drown** in.
the **deeper** you dive in, the more your lungs fill with air.

hide-and-seek.

are you settling for what's comfortable, or are you getting
what you deserve? ask yourself more intimate questions.
stop hiding in tight corners and blending in with the darkness.
dig deep into truth until it bleeds gold.

(who heals the healer? the healer heals the healer)

no one can heal you the way you can heal you,

and that's one of your greatest **superpowers**.

metamorphosis.

know that you are **magic**.

you are not meant to be the person that you were yesterday.

you are meant to be an extension of all the beautiful
things that you have experienced in life.

you are meant to be a much deeper, intricate ocean,
full of different hues and contrasts.

you are meant to evolve and outgrow the skin
that no longer keeps you warm.

you are meant to be whoever, or whatever you want to be.

you are meant to be authentic, true, and **colorful**.

Andrews McMeel Publishing
a division of Andrews McMeel Universal
1130 Walnut Street, Kansas City, Missouri 64106

www.andrewsmcmeel.com

21 22 23 24 25 BVG 10 9 8 7 6 5

ISBN: 978-1-4494-9937-2

Library of Congress Control Number: 2018951807

Cover design by HOLT. for NO PLATEAU Design

Editor: Patty Rice
Designer, Art Director: Julie Barnes
Production Editor: Elizabeth A. Garcia
Production Manager: Carol Coe

ATTENTION: SCHOOLS AND BUSINESSES
Andrews McMeel books are available at quantity discounts with
bulk purchase for educational, business, or sales promotional use.
For information, please e-mail the Andrews McMeel Publishing
Special Sales Department: specialsales@amuniversal.com.